MW00620324

Delgado's poetry comes at you from behind to whisper heart attacks disguised as love stories. Ditch Water plunges readers into murky depths of desire and dislocation, as this collection charts an intense journey strewn with utter fearlessness and grit. Delgado makes a strong contribution to contemporary queer Xicano poetics. His raw images grind their way into the bones, leaving teeth marks and maps of the desert. This book should come with a seatbelt.

T. Jackie Cuevas, Ph.D., Assistant Professor
Syracuse University

The desert flesh, in Delgado's poetry, is ripped open and oozing. Something murky accumulates here, like ditch water, in the in-between spaces that have not yet healed. The desert people who populate these poems, themselves carrying bone deep memories and displaying skin turned purple to the touch, reject our pity. They remind us that the ravaged desert flesh is their own and that ditch water, accumulated through the scarring of earth and flesh, and ingested for survival, is also an acquired taste. No apologies are necessary here. Delgado's poetry is dark, but its darkness gives us glimpses of what we need to see.

Ernesto Martínez, author of *On Making Sense: Queer Race Narratives of Intelligibility* and co-editor of *Gay Latino Studies: A Critical Reader*

The poems of Joseph Delgado's Ditch Water cut, tear, and rip time. Each untidy shred of a moment, scene, or image captures experience at its most electric, its most inviting. Unfamiliar odors in refrain, "that smell again," "the stink of early summer," and mysterious songs, "a moth/breaking its body against wind," "knees scraping against plaster," beckon the reader come closer. If not from the first page, you feel the speaker's "bones show through the skin." Reading leads to infatuation; Delgado arrives as every fence, every drop of air across tin roof tops, in grains of cornmeal and powdered milk. Stay the night with these poems, "night like a sick horse / stomping the dust into the ground." And awaken in their "dank sticky air."

Kristen Naca, author of *Bird Eating Bird*

DRIED WATER

DITCH WATER

JOSEPH DELGADO

Foreword by Rigoberto González

DITCH WATER

POEMS

Kórima Press

Copyright © 2013 Joseph Delgado

All rights reserved. No portion of this work may be reproduced, performed, recorded, copied or otherwise transmitted in any form or by any means without written permission from the author or publisher except for small excerpts for educational or journalistic purposes.

Credits:
"burning" previously appeared in different form in *Glyph Literary Magazine* of The College of Santa Fe, Spring 1999.

"never saw him again," "scrub," "broken shack," "arizona porn shop," previously appeared in *Joto: An Anthology of Queer Xicano & Chicano Poetry* (Kórima Press, 2012)

Cover Art: Marla Allison
Title: "9-11-01"
Medium: Acrylic and Mixed Media on Canvas
Dimensions: 48" X 36"
Date: 2001
www.marlaallison.com

Book Design: Lorenzo Herrera y Lozano

Published by Kórima Press
San Francisco, CA
www.korimapress.com

ISBN: 978-0-9889673-3-5

Dedicated to the Memory of Mi Tía

Rosella Baca

1958-1996

CONTENTS

FOREWORD

by Rigoberto González

The southwestern desert has two faces. The first is celebrated and romanticized on postcards and photographs--dispatches from the tourists who report back on the expansive blue sky, the pretty flowers and cacti that appear to pose for the camera, the soothing light that coats everything with peaceful surrender. Indeed, some days the desert is harmless like that. The second, more unsightly face of the desert is filled with shame and fear. It is therefore ushered away from the public eye, though this face sometimes peeks out through the headlines: violence, poverty, hunger, and death. Yes, there is cold in the desert. Yes, there is night. Sometimes the desert is brutal like that.

Only the true dweller can speak to the desert's brutality, and not as an indictment or a battle cry, but rather as an experience--the everyday reality of those who will live and die in the uncompromising landscape that has thrived long before it became inhabited, that will thrive long after it is emptied of people. What is left then? The bodies that cross paths with the heat. Their stories will carry with the wind and follow the last voice out of the land.

Such is the state of urgency and ephemerality of Joseph Delgado's debut collection of poems Ditch Water, a visceral, sensory journey through the today of a young male speaker who examines and articulates his immediate surroundings through the gritty, grainy desert lens. From the poem "ditch bank morning":

> i awoke with a mouthful
> of stars
> burning hot on my
> tongue like chile
>
> rotting dry red
> like snakes peeling their skin
> loose   untangled
> from the fresh wet
> the dank sticky air
>
> in this ditch   muddied jaw
>
> and ankles
>
> my body splits like a
> dead coyote in the summer

One of the more startling discoveries in Ditch Water is how the speaker's vocabulary remains within his reach, his favorite words are tongue, bone, thigh, skin and other body parts that mirror the desert's composition-- sand, water, light, wind, sun and moon. The young man's task then is to weave and press these entities together so that the desert imagery remains intimate with the human body. Thus, "sunrise like a/ battered woman/ rises over/ the heavy rock of mesa" and "her voice low like the hum/ of radiator hiss or a moth/ breaking its body against wind": this is the language of hard-won pronouncements, the small but telling glimpses of larger conflict.

Though Delgado writes about thirst and sun damage, there are other threats and afflictions made by the self or other people. This barrio community, "wind torn" and "dust chewed," so public beneath the glare of daylight, has its secret and not-so secret hurts: alcoholism, drug use, domestic abuse, and a downtrodden young man who must quench "the burning inside these ribs" with drunken lovers and "the hungers of nameless men" in cheap motels and porn shops. He finds his way through smell and sound and taste, the animal urges palpable in the quiet, on the restless sheets.

The speaker's search for solace, for the semblance of happiness or fulfillment, is what gives Ditch Water its substance and emotional center. Indeed, he is part of a troubled population that despite its economic hardship (or perhaps because of it) copes with purchased alcohol and sex. Yet the young man's queerness shifts the narrative, not into tragedy, but rather into agency--while others attempt to escape their bodies through everything from drug-numbness to suicide, he is attempting to transcend into a type of physical empowerment nearing enlightenment:

> i rise to heavy flesh
> the taste of heat dry skin, the taste of
> a moist tongue.   waist deep in darkness

> ...

> the plush of a violet stain under the skin
> pushed in again like man into man   sweat glazed jaws, unshaven
>
> i rise to the purple tongued moon
>
> i rise from this dirtied bed
> wipe the chalk white from my nose
> my lips, watch the rising sun light
> slip itself into the room.

The speaker's body survives like the desert, enduring bruise, wound, scar and stretch mark by absorbing it into its physical identity. There is no declaration of pain, though it is a painful story; there is no stepping out of the present tense, though the journey leaves behind a trail of carnage, evidence of scuffle and strife: "how many angels sent to tear/ this flesh away?"

Ditch Water is a raw, honest book that is unafraid to show visitors its darkness and shadows. It completes a portrait of a setting that has been limited to "natural beauty" at the expense of erasing its people and other less appealing dimensions. Delgado brings back complexity and gravity to a place that will outlive us all, though until then it is obligated to listen to each and every footfall, drink each tear like a drop of rain, silently witness the tiniest utterance of despair:

> holy mary mother of god
>
> pray for this skin
>   busted and stained

light washing the stink
from my belly

tongues stiffening in the wet dark

Beloved reader, beloved visitor, prepare yourself for a memorable anointing. Ditch Water is the baptismal font of Joseph Delgado's desert.

Rigoberto González
June 4, 2012
New York, NY

ACKNOWLEDGMENTS

I would foremost like to thank toda mi familia for their undying and unrelenting support of my writing and art; especially mi Tía Rosella Baca, may she rest in peace, for always supporting me in my youth; for mi primo John Turrietta for always having my back; and of course my parents for breathing life into me. I would also like to thank my good friend, Marla Allison, for always being a champion of my work and for her considerably deep friendship. I want as well to thank Lorenzo Herrera y Lozano for seeing something of value in my work and taking a chance on this barrio raised, rez living baboso.

DITCH
WATER

dirty

1.
the wind shook the dust
from the roof of this building
spit, root, and ash
>and the sky rose, full tongued
>over the ridge of my body
>falling apart

>how many angels sent to tear
>this flesh away?

2.
she knelt at my feet crying
praying, scrubbing the stains
from my thighs.
>*'la llorona did this'*
she mumbled, then
smacked the soiled sheets on the
tin wire out to dry
as i watched shadows crawl below the
bellies of saints, the flicker of wax
wet candles.

3.
sew these eyes shut
these orbs of dense brown
>like crushed junky powder
>like the sands of my birth,
clean this lengua of the grit, the
resin that so many have left.

4.

on the river i could smell the waters
       thick at my nose,
       scurrying across my chest,
           war beaten
       forest of salt-cedar
       forest of dark leaves,
like an ageless dust come
hunting my bones over hills
       and deserts
and mountains of stone.

5.

she raised the straight edge blade
to my throat, told me of the tecatos
       that would slip their
       fingers up her woolworth skirts
       bite her lip in the
       back of old chevys

'mi corazon de polvo'
yes this heart of dust come
       beating at the door
       like a drunk, come
       hollering for the wet smell
           that would fill him.

6.
this wind that ripples the skin
pulls me tight like guitar wood
and the chill running
through my weakened bones broken
twice over
crawling belly down under my
        flesh muscle
this air scissoring through my wet
darkness.

llano

that smell again
coiling around my limbs
licking at the sides
of my throat
        dirty dish water
        coyotes's old beer cans
        rattling in the
        breeze,
wet charcoal pit
        rain smothered,
        smelling raw
        like a silt licked rain
like those panties pressed
        hard against the face.
the smell of nylon and cheap
lipstick on the collar, burnt
dried plum colored blood,
like an oleander
tip seared red orange
like a sunset bursting open
through purple dark,
bloodied water seeping
across almond colored sheets
almond like flesh tearing
through dark indian skin,

and my hand trembling
grasping the glass of booze,
swirling brown,

and i can hear the
tecatos shuffling through
the leaves, fingering for
the needles that they
too will press to their bodies and
with a grin push through
olive skin, and stain,
a sucked kiss left bleeding,
a tear
a drop of metal, clank,
        split the thick silence

that smell again, that gin cedar smell
heavy, pressing its lips hard toothed
against the chest, against
the milkless breast of mine
nipple glowing gold brown,
shimmering bronze like
a juárez whore
beating her cracked teeth
against the cock of a borracho
that spits in her face,
        slurs cheap beer
        gurgling
        dirtied throat.

kitchen light

he split the sweat
from his back
arches in the kitchen light
the hiss of air conditioner
through the tangled
threads of smoke
fumed from mouth and tooth
        jaw unshaven

fumbling with newspapers yellowed
from the dry cold

his eyelids snapping closed
with the stretching of his skin
the darkened waters of
his body swirling
deep in his belly

as cigarette smoke
blossoms from his tongue

city bus

city bus shimmering
choking blue black fumes
        hot neon sun
        flickering flame along
        heated concrete and bones

they say la virgen comes
to this corner
snapping tongue and
rattle of wire and rotted seeds

her feet warm against the
sidewalk littered with spit
and ash
        and the smeared
        butt of heat split
        tobacco

the gurgling grind of
brakes and it's there
        rumbling flesh filled
        carrying the smog of sweat
across barrios   wind torn
        dust chewed

dying witch

she smells of camphor and cotton
skin reddened moist   sweat
        hot light slithering belly down
        through the alfalfa
        air sweet
heavy on skin

wrinkled and fat she wrestles her
old skin in the sheets
        bones clanking shuffling like
        a body coming undone

        she wants out
        of the creased gowns of
        aged flesh
        folded and bent

her thighs pulled and stretched
        heat filled gut swollen

she cries out 'dios mío'

her voice low like the hum of
radiator hiss or a moth
breaking its body against wind

hospital room

cough and hiss
drop and drip tubes

      tendrilled, tangled
into darkened veins

      body limp, cool
      unshaven in a dirty klieg light

the bloom of violets
in the inner arm,

          wrists like twigs
          bent in a heated wind

      soiled dirty sheets left
         wrinkled-pissed

the stench of old skin
hovers between metal and
porcelain

eyes glimmering like pennies

through the screen door

1.
i scrub the taste of copper from my tongue
this rag of blood red skin and fat
flapping against tooth and gum
and soured spit

clip the taste from the back of the throat
darkened swollen wet, cough
lungfull of ash

glimmer of sweat
on the edge of jaw
chip of moon heated bone

2.
im at the sink
panting like a fly-picked dog
hunger heavy stream of water
faucet crackling rusted raw

my chest swollen
dark filled
bones snapped muscle clean

3.
i watch la llorona through the screen door
scrubbing her thighs clean of
wind and river water
the stench of tamarisk salt on
        her fingertips.

nursing home dream

you couldnt eat
wrestled in your own skin
tangled cords and tubes and
dried spit on your face

      the blue moon light
slipped past your skirts and
knee high stockings
broke past your rotten teeth

and there your tongue
clicked to the sound of crickets

      and boys rolling cigarettes
down by the ditch
stinking of mud and crawfish

you couldnt move
strapped moaning in half sleep
the flies picking at your breasts
and wrinkled neck

      they found you jaw open
      wide eyed

clenched in panic and sleep and the sticky
night slipping from between your thighs
as the sunlight swallowed the sky

rusted morning

this lip split by fist and knuckle
bruises stitched to skin like tattoos
      barrio green shimmer and flake of
      old english on the chest

      the last mouthful of schlitz beer
gurgles
      down my throat as
lizard snap tails and tongues
in the bunch grass, glass littered,
glowing tecato brown
      in sunlight

      trailing tongue off of wet backs
and this back, bent, deboned
in the tomato field,   *la tierra del fuego*
aflame
where saints are entangled in barb wire
and crow bones

the dry hands of junipers dancing   steaming
in the wind

this wind heavy with grit and
burnt metal
      junky spoons needles   and busted veins
      dangling in the bathroom light

o.d. in june

almond tile
chipped

          rubber
          metal in arm   shooting at

collapsed healed thin darkness   chasing

i can taste the tub plaster,
      chalk staleness at
      the back of the throat   thumb print in the eyelids   faucet

drain   drain   taking hair and grit down to
public waste pools   feather light smoke

      smudging thighs   where did she go?

window
door
closet

'tía'

tipped glass of cigarette butts
summer heat pasted loosely on walls-bed-newspaper print
    wrapping that brown powder   camel teeth crushed
        boiled thick
syrup filled syringe skimming the   bluegreen threads of veins

the clank of spoon dropping from wrist   baby bone
cutting pink skin   watered lungs   half-clad
    slipping
        to   the   soiled   floor

    they peeled her wide open
held in their hands her liver
    kidneys   drained her of that river
        that stink
    the incision on her belly   feeling finger way through wombless inside uterus
stripped   dried plum flaps of tissue,
        and the boy i am dropping a coin from
        these june warm hands

sister

she placed her hands
      on her ears
   to not listen   to not know
               father beating   mother
                                     the clank of dresser

               body flung against wood paneled
                       wall.

she covered her ears *'dont believe'*

'dont believe in what' i asked

with a dry mouth   the
           lamplight   splintering on my   tongue

               she wiped her mouth, stained
lips   *'dont believe in me'*

american senator

he stumbled   with the
      buttons on my jeans

          his face marked by age, by the heat of
          some midwestern sun, by the shame of
          hotel rooms

he said i reminded him of his son
wanted to sketch his fingers along my washed thighs
      wanted to be pushed, face first into the
          pillows, wanted to feel me

      wanted to bite my tongue in two

now at this pay phone i try to call
      hoping he doesnt answer, hoping
his wife picks up, so i can say   *yes, i know.*

burning

1.
i cut the moonlight
        from your unshaven throat

        with my tongue

my teeth,   my skin wrapped jaw.

mother sat   in the kitchen bending spoons
under a moth light, a light   flickering
                scratching starched colored shadows

into the walls.   the   creases of her face.

        your naked thighs, gathering the

blueblack cold, the cold thick at our chests
and   arms.

you strummed my rib cage, felt you teething
on my blue veined wrist,

     a song, the crack of her
     the snap of a child's bone under

i could hear mother singing,
voice like a snap of bull's eyelid,
his father's fist

2.
     i lick the inside of your ear
thinking of how i never told you i used to kiss my mother,
     in the haze of bathrooms, the back seat of my grandfathers model t

how i lifted my cousins' skirts above their waists, pushed through the tight dark skin, pushed
     through sour flesh, and how i knew, yes, how i never wanted to go back.

3.
     and as you lie next to me
     twisting scoured metal, the metal of your bones,
mother still humming,
     i smoke to remember those times

i think of all the things i never told you,   these smells,   with me pushing into

and when you ask, i will only smother you with these fluids,
you

smother you with the burning
inside these ribs.

22

what the ditch water showed me

fumbling through the
mud of ditches   i feel the wind
eating at my shoulders
the lungs pressing against their

cage   their   dark chamber of bone   like

blood cooling   the dizziness

antelope
burning in the summer fields,   their skins heating taut
like rawhide, horses digging their lips
into grass, cattle tracks, shivering blind

dizzy like when you fucked me mad, bare bodied in
the summer, on the porch where i imagined your   mother could see us.

where   she   could watch from her

sofa

where you pressed me into the shadows and
stuffed my mouth   with the

                                              passing beyond the
          sounds of trains   through
cedar, the night   i sifted
                              the salts of your body

                          fumbling   through the ditch to find the
broken boned   sparrow, the rabid dog digging
                through the   trash heaps,
                smelling of bowels   blackening
          the thick night   pulling my hair,   twisting

                into me,   like you, like

horse-fly   pricking flesh   the smell of

melon, cut fresh   clean on the
chopping board,   a mother closing her eyes to her son,
                    lips stained   with the milk of another.

thanksgiving

i rise to the purple tongued moon

rise to the dust settling in the
half-eaten light
the naked heat of radiator
scratches the arch of my back, skin
            loosening, then tightening

the shadows do not move
stitched silent to these
scotchtaped trailer walls, the sounds of
            a woman pissing in the sink down the hall
            knees scraping against the plaster

i rise to heavy flesh
the taste of heat dry skin, the taste of
a moist tongue.   waist deep in the darkness

            deep in these skins that i smelt with my tongue
            salts crackling, crackling like my sister rinsing water
            over the bruises of her arms, thin tubes of metal
pushed through, then pulled   then pushed again   used

            the plush of a violet stain under the skin
pushed in again like man into man sweat glazed jaws, unshaven

i rise to the purple tongued moon

i rise from this dirtied bed
wipe the chalk white from my nose
my lips, watch the rising sun light
slip itself into the room.

saturday outside town

the moonlight thick at my thighs

i lie in this cheap motel,
thinned men begging to be
beaten outside,
        outside in that heavy summer air

       their bodies opening
closing   thumb nail
       pressed deep inside

pockmarked faces gleaming
in the haze of cigarette smoke,
        fading headlights.

      a warm breeze tightening
      around the
jaw of each man,

      each man   without a grin
each night, gathering in the heated darkness
      drawn by hunger
      the hungers of nameless men.

      and when they close their eyes to the slicing
within, they become faceless.

here angels burn deep inside the flesh, like cinders,
      burnt hunger,
and through the cracked windows,
      the dawn light slowly rising to my tongue.

cruisin'

tonguing the darkness
  damp flesh   cloth   sunrise like a battered
                rises over
         woman
    the heavy rock of mesa
    blazes like fire to my skin ripped
    skin   from bone

smearing white into the nose
  bursting at the veins insown
       heat

    heart muscle burning

how many times

  the dark musk of
   a mother's sweat soaked girdle
       casts its shadow

  across the age fatted breasts.

DELGADO

girls with their   razors pitched to the tongue   lifted to the dull

glow of a   dusted bulb   i can smell their skins   stretching across

the magnolia stained   bones,   across   the blood filled tissue of their loins

how many times

scream   howl   glazed naked, chalk dust fusing to the lips

boys whispering their names, never leaving a number   never wanting to kiss   only

smack down the waters of the body, flush   dark holes with the musk with

the veined flesh of fingers   screaming   *i could do this all day*   *i could burst in you*

i want you

arizona porn shop

i push you down
jab my tongue down in you
stuff you with my fluids, my spit
my cum swirling mad wild untamed in
your darkness

mijo, papi, nameless man peering through
the mucked hole in the stall wall
green light hums with the thumping of your thighs
clattering of belt buckles
and quarters, the stirring of
video clips cast about your eyes

suck me you say
suck this
and i take tongue, wetness, haired flesh
and swallow

hombre, viejo, spines
arching in the tv light
arching to the spasms of body, flesh
and old odors,
crumpling of paper towels wiping

the thighs clean, boxer shorts
stuck to my balls
stuck to the waist

pull it you say
toque mi verga you shout
in the bland dark
tasting of sweat and blood
and shit, that stench of
young men
pulling at themselves
sticking cocks through the night
the holes tighten

and you bend under me
bend in the heat of my sweat
the heat of my body snapping
you in half
cutting the urge from under your skin.

summer comes

the stink of early summer
wind scratches my face
slices across the bridge of my nose
like a saw, the chiseling of blades
against the hot blooded bones

the chip of night moon
slipping down my throat
like hair and grit down
scoured metal drains   unscrubbed tubs
shaking porcelain dust like
coke, off the wings
scissoring through the feathery air
a sky burnt black, kneaded
dull   numb

my head pounding like flames
against the pine, smacking the
flesh pulp down, gurgling the
smoke, tendrilling aimlessly up into
the thin braided air

and this wind
wraps like a gauze around
my body, my skin busted
open like a war-wounded vato
shaking mad in the barrio
the smack of muscle and bone
tin roofs rattling
like eyeless snakes
shaking the skin
from their coiled bodies

as i shuck the heat
from my bones.

broken shack

i remember when you bit my tongue
as i pushed my fingers through
your hair, pomade glowing
under the street light, that same
street light where your mother
pulled her dress up
showed me the folds of her loins
and the smell of cheap perfume
and gas station cigars
filled the air like a
gathering of flies

and them too
buzzing around like a hangover
landing on your tattooed chest
my spittle tracing down your
nipples, over your neck

you cut my lip with your teeth
called me a puto
but i couldnt stop grabbing your cock
and didnt you want it?
didnt you want to push into me, belly down
on the floor?
pushing   harder
the musty air
hot
our sweat entangling

and you cum on my stomach
you push your mouth to my jaw
my ear
and you say
'te quiero
i want your...your smell...'

        and i push your tongue
        from my mouth
        button my jeans   leaving you
        naked in the mojave night

barrio wind

i listen to the hot barrio wind
curl its tongue over the
tin roofs, rattle ristras and
coat hangers dangling from
ranflas

gasp of engine gurgling
with oil and sweat
this wind that sucks on my neck,
stitches itself to the
underside of my chin

and i hear it, slicing across the
faces of vatos talking shit
spitting jim bean and fuming with
smoke
and the taste of salt cedar
entangles in my teeth, and
pushes its fingers down my throat

i listen to the barrio wind
slip through the chainlink fences
hissing like the sound of woman shucking sweet corn
and a dog licks shadows
from the sticky fur
as i stumble through the empty
fields of glass and sun yellowed grass,
wiping the hot light
from my mouth

neighborhood song

the sun pulls me,
drags my body of bones
through the cracked asphalt roads,
beaten by the thick heat,
beaten leant over sinks
like girls getting finger fucked
in cheap best western motel rooms,
the stink of old wallpaper
and off-white plaster
brillo burnt tip   inhale
the throat pulses with
the heated smoke

she pulls her panties
over her knees as she
pisses in a toilet that
wont flush that wont
take her yellowed fluid down
that sears through the
ceramic silence burning on
tongues of young boys jacking off
to their daddys playboys
bones shown through the skin.

under the skin

i can taste the fat of the spring heat
between my teeth, the gritted taste of
smog and manteca smoke
stumbling through the alleyways
slicing across the faces of
black boys peeling light from their skins

and the tecato shaves his scarred face
cleans, foam scraped, dirt
soap, hair floating in the grey water
and the roses, them too shimmering
along the arms, legs, throat
the browned rose color
staining veins, dark green bands twisted under
the skin

i can hear the lizards snapping their eyelids
shut to the hot wind, thick, sticky at the
underside of my chin
under the pit of my arms
the swelling sweat salty stuck to my brow
stitched close to my unshaved chest
and i pull the thick
strands of
santa ana wind from my mouth, my gums stained
like a wild dog

and again the tecato shivers
in his tired, skin
again rattles the spoons
to mark the sliver of shade
slipping
through the green darkness

witch

sunrise

like a beaten body
slips over the edge
of my hip

      it cuts across her face
      as she rinses the blood
      from her thighs

            panties and sheets soaking
            in the tub

she says *i once killed a baptist man*
as she sponges the copper stains from
her stubbled skin

day dream

the snap of
bones shucked from mud blackened skin
and a moth shakes its
paper wings in the stretched dark
of a room   hot, sweat brimming
          flooding each pore with the spittle
          of wet dreams

          my body stinks of bear skin and
          trout bones

i can hear it in the alleys, the streets of this
stuccoed barrio reeking of pig fat and
wood smoke   the bruising of
jaws and arms   boiled syrup shot straight into
threaded veins

crawling belly down under the skin
under the skin blossoming, plush, metal stained
and i wade in the sheets

the air sticky at my thighs and i smell
it burning in the grit littered roads, burning
in the fields, calling from the thickets of weeds
and grasses, calling from beneath these skins

          my body stinks of cornmeal
          and powder milk

and the moon licks the dampness from this
bed, broken, crumbling in the early morning shadows
creasing and bending in the street light, the lamp shivering
hot white in calm night, this night
snapping my bones in two, gathering

the stink of my sweat

scrub

i wash my hands
    of the mud
    shards of wet light

    tattooed along my
    arms

glimmering   the cleanser smell
                reaches the edge of

          my chin

    that old odor
    the scent of a boy masturbating
    into the water

into the sliced light. alone.

      that scent of a boy
      tracing the edge
    of his thighs
      milk that had
      run down his legs

    a man who had sucked the skin raw.
i wash my hands where a tongue had cracked
silently.

dirty sheets

he shifted his skin
in the cold dark

      his veins numbed
            collapsed
            the wet green
            bruises
      extended to a moonless
      night

he licked the stretched skin
of my belly   the
      hairs on his chin
      catching the faint
      light of
      cigarettes   burning

or was it a car?
a flash in the thick
      cold of winter

our   wind blistered lips
      cracking breaking loose

      split open to the cool
            spittle of two men.

he pressed his thumb
          deep inside
          warm
the wild grasses
          howling at our ankles
          pulling   calling

the wind scratching, gnawing
at my body
          flesh sliding in and out of flesh

ash

i licked the ash from your
sun swollen thigh
      tasted the mud colored
      shadows slipping beneath
      your skin

shimmering pale clay

        sand stained

     this skin beaten against
rocks and heavy hipped
river currents
       i smother the
       moonlight on my chest
         and belly

the fatted belly gutted
wide open as
rain fed peach split open
in the hot barrio wind

the smell of burnt mulberry
and junky metal clanking
like the dog next door
barking into the
heated afternoon and that
buzzing like a broken radiator
chincharras rattling their seven
year wings

and mother hanging the
last sweat soaked
sheets out to dry
and the boys down the
street comparing scars
and wind beaten muscles

late night lover

you came to my window   late
with a can of beer in
your hand, you call me *amor*
your chest twitching sweated under your
muscle shirt

i pull the shoes from your feet,
peel your creased jeans,
your darkened legs dangling
to the side,
push you over   sleep
i stay up all night scrubbing
beer and vomit
from carpets   cleanser

spilling over my knuckles and
i curse myself for doing this
again   no rest
you in drunken sleep, kicking
frothing   through
the night like a sick horse
stomping the dust into the ground
grinding grit, my bones
twice broken
on a night like this

the moonlight stabbed
through the venetian blinds
cut across my face   sharp white
blade slicing the sleep
from my heavy eyes   paring
the dark fed skin

this apple pulp flesh
the sounds of junkies stumbling
through the alley dark
clanking needles and beer bottles
you breathe deep sleep slumped on my
dirtied bed
as sirens whimper through oil slicked streets
barrio breeze shakes
past mulberry and elm

i can smell gunpowder
settling on the shoulders
of old men spitting and
drinking warm schlitz
i think of abuelo sitting with
his scared heart gulping beer
in the sanjo night
whistling old war songs
singing of chihuahua and agave
cutting the silence with
a clank of empty
beer can

i can hear the barrio breeze entangling
in the snarls of
chained dogs, in the heavy folds
of your body slipping in the sheets.

a song

a body of smoke
wisps through the
chainlink fence as a
viejita rolls tortillas in the
yellowed light   her hands
wind bitten, worn raw,
sliced open like the
earth, like the moonlight
through the salt cedar

dawn

the blue slipped
from the skin as the moon
bent herself open, bone
broken, jaw bruised
        busted
split open like sheep
skin in the early morning
january cold, splintered,
sucked clean, husked from
the wheat colored
film, this pelt
unlit sweated in a room
darkened with the stench
of wet dreams and cheap
wine

the rain comes

i can smell it

                    the rain
          choking on dust on those
          cracked rock cluttered
              slopes

where your name is carved
                chalk white
     wings   flutes   batting
                the grit filled air

where wet tongues clatter toothless
     for clouds that tint the

         sky grey dark   like in between
                       your thighs

i can smell it   the rain
              smeared into your skin
              mojave they whisper
     those of clay and tattoo
           of rabbit pelt and fish smell
           their jaws striped blue

breasts glimmering copper in the
salted sunlight   the rain smothering
this fatted body of mine   stinking of tobacco
and uncooked breath   the rain coming for this
      coyote skin

sunday

the smell of tortillas
fills that dark house
        wood slat   cracked
        chipped paint

father leans over porcelain sink
    slicing light from fish bones
    pulled flailing
    wild   mad   from

    waters   shucked from
                grey skies
                bled of light

    the comal heated black
    on match lit stove
                masa rising on the
                counter

        watching the bones flex under
        the skin of mother's hand
        through the flour dust

ditch bank morning

i awoke with a mouthful
        of stars
                        burning hot on my
                        tongue like chile

        rotting dry red
                        like snakes peeling their skin
                                        loose   untangled
        from the fresh wet
                        the dank sticky air

        in this ditch   muddied jaw

                        and ankles

                        my body splits like a
                        dead coyote in the summer

                        heat blood splattered
        burnt on the roadway
                                        stinking like uncooked
                                        moon

trying to score

a colorless wind sews itself
into my heavy thighs   sweated
          slacked skin unthreaded
under a silver blue moon
          a moon howling mad

          like tía rosella, that hot barrio night
          train track junky heat sizzling
                    tip of breast
                    broken vein

          mad running barefoot through
          the asphalt the darkness
          smelling of manteca and oiled paños

calling out from shivering corners
          for the tecato powder
          mad clank of metal   the tearing of
          skin, a garden of violets spreading
          along the inner arm

and i gnaw on tobacco licked wind
as i snuff the burning cigarette
          from the open mouth of an aunt
          bent at the couch heat crackling
          in the veins of her wet back

neon glow

busted light
flickering in the dirty
dishwater, beer cans
clanking under foot
deer bones rinsed clean

snapped under heavy foot
jaws cracking with tobacco smoke
and whiskey
cum stuck to my belly

cedar fires smoldering
smoked, wet stink
wood flame gnawed
moon light biting the
pink skin of necks

hotel neon glowing
dry blue

song of the old road

bending metal light
burnt tip of cigarette

i think of riding in the back of chevys passing
joints sipping cheap beer stolen
from tíos fridge
that dull taste at the back of the throat
someones tongue pressed in between teeth

and the glow of traffic lights
crosses my face
the smell of alamo and yerba buena
slips past my chin

highway motel

he stunk of raw potatoes
and old tin
        the lacquered skin
heavy pockmarked

        in a gritty neon glow

bed sheets rippled still
like dirty pond water

bleached white like
        teeth gnawed

buffalo bones
        and wind smacked
corn husks

his breath coiling up
        through the coffee colored teeth
and busted jaw
        cold like a dog
run rawed smooth flat
on the blacktop of long highways
busted open   rubber rutted

the smell of beer

down at the las palomas
        bar

                in the sticky yellow
        haze of dusted light
        and smoke

tecatos swarm mad
        needle prodded

        in the flicker of
        bathroom lights

dirty jokes inked on
        stall doors

toilet rim glowing
        rum colored

mouthful of spit
        and stink

of tar and metal

snap of vein under
winter dried skin.

sitting with a whore

watching
old apache
      drunk stumbling
dick hard and dirty

central ave. gleaming
exhaust full
     shimmer of
     late moon glow

and she offers to bite
your neck

pulling panties off
     in the unpeeled
  banana dark

at the back of the bar

a jaw busted
    wide open

the buzz of jukebox

    and drunks

        pissing in the autumn
        licked dust

        skin pressed against
        skin

stinking of vodka
    and woodsmoke

        white light thick
            syrup
        fills my darkness

prayers

1.
panting at the window
the wasp wrapped in
light

2.
a wind hard and frozen
stumbles into the yard
bruises leaves and a
            wisp of sand

3.
i braided yucca
            and anise
into my hair
            tip of tongue
    slashed sweet
            and bitter

petal white unstitching
in the moist heat
            hidden behind the jaw

mud and clay caked to
            my knees, ankles
rock heavy, swollen

4.
flutter flick
          wing
broken on the
window screen

dust

5.
ashes to ashes
wings to fire
          feather smoldering
          with fat
and river water

6.
i will scrub the
sweat salt from my tongue

and split the
skin at my thighs

                    scalding water

          burnt steam

and clean this scent
from my bones

7.
and the wasp gathers
wingful of wet light
whimpering

      as wind tangles
      in the heavy limbs of
      mesquite trees.

at night

wake to find the cold
licking feverishly at my
thighs

      rain swollen

thick with fat and
twisted bone

my body pockmarked
with moonlight
      and the stink
of corn

      bitter root tongue
      dried
broken like wood slipped
open by frost.

act of contrition

1.
a eucalyptus tree
gathers the dusk to
its body   its hardened
skin crumbling brown

        muck in the overtilled
        dust

the bushes
heavy with cotton
twigs extended wind bruised

and an old tecato
sits in the shade
peeling back the rose bush
tattoo searching for the
dark green threads that
will fill his gut

soothe the twisted muscles
under their wrap of dry skin.
burn in the pit of
his heart sleep

and the last dusty light
drops from trees tangles in
the moss green of ink stains and
pockmarks
        a droplet of blood bending into shadows

2.
hail mary full of grace
wombs gone empty
taketh this body raw
this body unburnt, skinless
and whole

3.
i dig my finger deeper
deeper into that darkness
a sour taste on my tongue

4.
and the wind beats its fist
raw against the trees, palms
bent like girls in hotel rooms

and the fields of alfalfa
stretch like a green skin
unburnt bones of mojaves

stir in the damp earth
as the grinding of piston
and motor churn the salted earth

5.
holy mary mother of god

pray for this skin
          busted and stained

light washing the stink
from my belly

tongues stiffening in the wet dark

6.
and the tecato
rinse his mouth with the
cheap gin
          mouthful of moths
          and dirty winds

his stomach
empty   cracked
          swirling slacked

in a pit of empty blue blackness

the sun blushes
          crawls behind mountains
of stone and sheep bones

          as the metal tube
          slips quiet into the loosened
          skin.

never saw him again

smoking now, cigarette tar
stuck to my jaw i remember
stripping our clothes off
      in the back of your car
      the smell of beer cans
      and weed pressed against
         the seats

you jab your tongue into my mouth
     dry   bite the edge of lip,

i remember tearing the fogged light
from your open chest with my
teeth blackened   yellowed with
spit   as you howled, grunted,
flapped naked and fat
in the dark of the backseat

you fumed mad like a froth
mouthed horse   spitting wildly
in the unsettled dust and smell,

i remember as i strike this match
     open flame

how i left you asleep and
peeled open, how i never
told you my name.

dishwater

she sliced melon
in the waning sun
cut meaty green flesh,
knife slipping through pulp
like a wind through a
field slipping past nopales
and calf bones,

sheep sweated dead
trampling in dust

and she wiped the dirty
dishwater on her brow

as a father beat a son
by the shed, the glow
of tomato on the lips
a tooth rattled
            came loose

knuckles bone white
whipping through skin
and panties   fingernails
broken, dulled
            chipped against
walls and old beds

she fans her breasts
            damp with sweat

pushes the newsprint down her
bra   her tongue licking the
film of want from her lips

and the sunday light
comes crashing through
windows
          watching the oleander
          glow hot

that smell

i can smell tangerine and
cheap lipstick
      on his neck, dark brown
      sun eaten

chewed by winds
full of cold
      ice, slicing through
wool coats and
      green veins

he flares his nostrils
      as burnt tobacco
      flutters between teeth
      and rot bleached gums

a skin stretched
marked, unstitched
      glowing lazy green
like unripened mango

      old english glimmering in the
      lamplight

as wind howls
past fly picked screens
and dusted glass

      bent wires and rusted
      fences

he stretched his body over
sweat stained mattress

      the odor of skin and
      newsprint

he watches the tv light
flicker on the walls

as the neighbor lady is
beaten against a heavy dresser

      a heavy fist
      warming the jaw.

the neighbor girl

as we kindle fire
in this old blackened stove
smelling of cedar and

pine sap

a girl tries to cut herself
in her room
slipping dull razor blade
against pink skin,

        veins green slicing
        under the surface

she can taste copper on her
tongue

        as her mother sucks
        on pipas and cigarettes

the dull thud of coca swimming in
veins and her naked
bent over a sink
        a man scared by light
        and bar fights

slams into her with hunger

as we watch the fire snap and
twist with black smoke

OTHER KÓRIMA PRESS TITLES

Amorcito Maricón
      by Lorenzo Herrera y Lozano

Brazos, Carry Me
      by Pablo Miguel Martínez

Empanada: A Lesbiana Story en Probaditas
      by Anel I. Flores

Las Hociconas: Three Locas with Big Mouths and Even Bigger Brains
      by Adelina Anthony

Joto: An Anthology of Queer Xicano & Chicano Poetry
      edited by Lorenzo Herrera y Lozano

Tragic Bitches: An Experiment in Queer Xicana & Xicano Performance Poetry
      by Adelina Anthony, Dino Foxx, and Lorenzo Herrera y Lozano

When the Glitter Fades
      by Dino Foxx